STRIVE

PRAYERS

AND

MEDITATIONS

FOR

YOUTH

BELLWOOD
PRESS®

WILMETTE, ILLINOIS

Bellwood Press
401 Greenleaf Avenue, Wilmette, Illinois 60091

25 24 23 22   4 3 2 1

Cover design by Carlos Esparza
Book design by Patrick Falso

ISBN 978-1-61851-216-1

Strive that your actions day by day
may be beautiful prayers. Turn towards God,
and seek always to do that which is right and noble.

—'Abdu'l-Bahá[1]

CONTENTS

Introduction...1

Where do these Prayers and Writings
Come From? 5

Giving Thanks 9

Trust in God 13

Spiritual Growth 17

Strength 23

Love 27

Joy..31

Difficulties 35

Protection 39

CONTENTS

Healing 45

Forgiveness 49

Justice 53

Unity 55

Service 63

Arts & Sciences 67

Children 71

Parents 75

Prayers Specifically for Girls 79

For those who have Passed Away 81

Short Obligatory Prayer 83

Glossary 85

Notes 95

Bibliography 103

INTRODUCTION

What is prayer and why do we pray? Prayer is a way for us to commune with God. We can do that by reading words such as the ones collected in this book. We can pray for help during difficult times, we can pray for the health of our family and friends, and we can pray as a way of giving thanks for all that we are grateful for. In the same way that food gives us sustenance and energy, prayer and meditation can feed our souls and give us spiritual nourishment.

However, prayer can be much more than that. The title of this book comes from the following words of 'Abdu'l-Bahá: "Strive that your actions day by day may be beautiful prayers." This is an interesting and unusual concept. It seems to suggest that prayer isn't just about sitting quietly and reading or reciting words. It seems to imply that actions can be prayers.

But what does that mean? Maybe anything we do in a spirit of love and devotion and kindness can be thought of as a type of prayer. What would our lives look like if we thought of our daily actions as prayers? What are some actions we could think about in this way? Helping a friend overcome a challenge, being kind to someone we don't know, playing a musical instrument, creating a piece of artwork, . . . If it's a matter of the spirit in which we do things, then the possibilities are endless.

The period of youth is a potent time of change, growth, and energy. When we are young, we have the power to transform not just our own reality, but to shape the destiny of the entire planet. And prayer is a tool that can elevate our efforts.

Some of the verses collected here are prayers that can help us reach out to God, and some of them are meditative passages that can help us reflect on life, with all of its ups and downs. If we make prayer and meditation a part of our daily routine—in our thoughts, words, and actions—we can grow spiritually, we can feel closer to God, and we can add a whole other dimension to our lives. It isn't always easy to find the time and the right frame of mind to do this, but we can try a little each day and see where it takes us.

We can strive.

WHERE DO THESE PRAYERS AND WRITINGS COME FROM?

The verses collected in this book come from the Bahá'í Faith. The Bahá'í Faith is a worldwide religious community that believes that all people belong to one human family, that there is one God, and that all the major religions of the world are like chapters in one evolving book. In this way, from a Bahá'í perspective, there is just one religion, which has had many different names as it has been updated throughout history. Some of these names include Buddhism, Hinduism, Zoroastrianism, Judaism, Christianity, and Islam. There are other, older ones, but the names have been lost to time.

Each religion was established by a Prophet, or Messenger of God, Who brought guidance that was suited to the time in which They appeared.

Each one built upon the teachings of the previous religion, but established a new one to help humanity mature and advance. The Bahá'í Faith is the latest of these religions, or, to put it another way, it is the latest chapter in this story. It was established less than 200 years ago in the middle of the nineteenth century by Bahá'u'lláh, Whose name means *the Glory of God*. Bahá'u'lláh's teachings are designed to bring about peace, harmony, and unity on planet Earth.

Many of the words in this book come directly from Bahá'u'lláh, the Messenger of God for today. There are also a few passages from another Messenger of God called the Báb, Whose name means *the Gate*. The Báb lived at the same time as Bahá'u'lláh, and His role was to prepare people for the coming of Bahá'u'lláh and the establishment of the Bahá'í Faith. The other name you will see throughout these pages is 'Abdu'l-Bahá, which means *Servant of the Glory*. 'Abdu'l-Bahá was the son of Bahá'u'lláh, and he looked after the Bahá'í Faith after his father's passing. He was not a Messenger of God, but is considered to be the perfect exemplar of the Faith's teachings. Verses from his prayers, writings, and talks are included here as well.

Today, all over the world, Bahá'ís are working to build communities based on the principles and teachings of Bahá'u'lláh, inviting their friends and neighbors to join them in their efforts. From junior youth groups, children's classes, and devotional gatherings, to study circles and service projects, there has never been a more exciting time to get involved.

GIVING THANKS

Ponder ye in your hearts the grace and the blessings of God and render thanks unto Him at eventide and at dawn.

—Bahá'u'lláh[1]

Praise be to Thee, O Lord my God, for guiding me unto the horizon of Thy Revelation and for causing me to be mentioned by Thy Name. I beseech Thee, by the spreading rays of the Daystar of Thy providence and by the billowing waves of the Ocean of Thy mercy, to grant that my speech may bear a trace of the influence of Thine own exalted Word, attracting thereby the realities of all created things. Powerful art Thou to do what Thou willest through Thy wondrous and incomparable Utterance.

—Bahá'u'lláh[2]

Do you realize how much you should thank God for His blessings? If you should thank Him a thousand times with each breath, it would not be sufficient because God has created and trained you. He has protected you from every affliction and prepared every gift and bestowal. Consider what a kind Father He is. He bestows His gift before you ask.

—'Abdu'l-Bahá[3]

Become ye as the birds who offer Him their thanks, and in the blossoming bowers of life chant ye such melodies as will dazzle the minds of those who know. Raise ye a banner on the highest peaks of the world, a flag of God's favor to ripple and wave in the winds of His grace; plant ye a tree in the field of life, amid the roses of this visible world, that will yield a fruitage fresh and sweet.

—'Abdu'l-Bahá[4]

Wherefore, thank ye God for setting upon your heads the crown of glory everlasting, for granting unto you this immeasurable grace.

The time hath come when, as a thank-offering for this bestowal, ye should grow in faith and constancy as day followeth day, and should draw ever nearer to the Lord, your God, becoming magnetized to such a degree, and so aflame, that your holy melodies in praise of the Beloved will reach upward to the Company on high; and that each one of you, even as a nightingale in this rose garden of God, will glorify the Lord of Hosts, and become the teacher of all who dwell on earth.

—'Abdu'l-Bahá[5]

TRUST IN GOD

God is sufficient unto me; He verily is the All-sufficing! In Him let the trusting trust.

—Bahá'u'lláh[1]

Praised be Thou, O Lord my God! Sanctify mine eye, and mine ear, and my tongue, and my spirit, and my heart, and my soul, and my body, and mine entire being from turning unto anyone but Thee. Give me then to drink from the cup that brimmeth with the sealed wine of Thy glory.

—Bahá'u'lláh[2]

Say: God sufficeth all things above all things, and nothing in the heavens or in the earth but God sufficeth. Verily, He is in Himself the Knower, the Sustainer, the Omnipotent.

—The Báb[3]

O Lord! Unto Thee I repair for refuge, and toward all Thy signs I set my heart.

O Lord! Whether traveling or at home, and in my occupation or in my work, I place my whole trust in Thee.

Grant me then Thy sufficing help so as to make me independent of all things, O Thou Who art unsurpassed in Thy mercy!

Bestow upon me my portion, O Lord, as Thou pleasest, and cause me to be satisfied with whatsoever Thou hast ordained for me.

Thine is the absolute authority to command.

—The Báb[4]

O Thou beloved of my heart and soul! I have no refuge save Thee. I raise no voice at dawn save in Thy commemoration and praise. Thy love encompasseth me and Thy grace is perfect. My hope is in Thee.

O God, give me a new life at every instant and bestow upon me the breaths of the Holy Spirit at every moment, in order that I may remain steadfast in Thy love, attain unto great felicity, perceive the manifest light and be in the state of utmost tranquility and submissiveness.

Verily, Thou art the Giver, the Forgiver, the Compassionate.

—'Abdu'l-Bahá[5]

SPIRITUAL GROWTH

Create in me a pure heart, O my God, and renew a tranquil conscience within me, O my Hope! Through the spirit of power confirm Thou me in Thy Cause, O my Best-Beloved, and by the light of Thy glory reveal unto me Thy path, O Thou the Goal of my desire! Through the power of Thy transcendent might lift me up unto the heaven of Thy holiness, O Source of my being, and by the breezes of Thine eternity gladden me, O Thou Who art my God! Let Thine everlasting melodies breathe tranquility on me, O my Companion, and let the riches of Thine ancient countenance deliver me from all except Thee, O my Master, and let the tidings of the revelation of Thine incorruptible Essence bring me joy, O Thou Who art the most manifest of the manifest and the most hidden of the hidden!

—Bahá'u'lláh[1]

O my Lord! Make Thy beauty to be my food, and Thy presence my drink, and Thy pleasure my hope, and praise of Thee my action, and remembrance of Thee my companion, and the power of Thy sovereignty my succorer, and Thy habitation my home, and my dwelling-place the seat Thou hast sanctified from the limitations imposed upon them who are shut out as by a veil from Thee.

Thou art, verily, the Almighty, the All-Glorious, the Most Powerful.

—Bahá'u'lláh[2]

He is God! O God my God! Bestow upon me a pure heart, like unto a pearl.

—'Abdu'l-Bahá[3]

O compassionate God! Thanks be to Thee for Thou hast awakened and made me conscious. Thou hast given me a seeing eye and favored me with a hearing ear, hast led me to Thy kingdom and guided me to Thy path. Thou hast shown me the right way and caused me to enter the ark of deliverance. O God! Keep me steadfast and make me firm and staunch. Protect me from violent tests and preserve and shelter me in the strongly fortified fortress of Thy Covenant and Testament. Thou art the Powerful. Thou art the Seeing. Thou art the Hearing.

O Thou the Compassionate God. Bestow upon me a heart which, like unto a glass, may be illumined with the light of Thy love, and confer upon me thoughts which may change this world into a rose garden through the outpourings of heavenly grace.

Thou art the Compassionate, the Merciful. Thou art the Great Beneficent God.

—'Abdu'l-Bahá[4]

O Lord!

Plant this tender seedling in the garden of Thy manifold bounties, water it from the fountains of Thy loving-kindness and grant that it may grow into a goodly plant through the outpourings of Thy favor and grace.

Thou art the Mighty and the Powerful.

—'Abdu'l-Bahá[5]

He is the Most Glorious!

O my merciful Lord! This is a hyacinth which hath grown in the garden of Thy good pleasure and a twig which hath appeared in the orchard of true knowledge. Cause it, O Lord of bounty, to be refreshed continually and at all times through Thy vitalizing breezes, and make it verdant, fresh and flourishing through the outpourings of the clouds of Thy favors, O Thou kind Lord!

Verily Thou art the All-Glorious.

—'Abdu'l-Bahá[6]

O Thou kind Lord!

Grant that these trees may become the adornment of the Abhá Paradise. Cause them to grow through Thy celestial bounty. Make them fresh and verdant and besprinkle them with heavenly dewdrops. Attire them with robes of radiant beauty and crown their heads with gorgeous blossoms. Adorn them with goodly fruit and waft over them Thy sweet savors.

Thou art the Bestower, the All-Loving, the Most Radiant, the Most Resplendent.

—'Abdu'l-Bahá[7]

O Thou Lord of wondrous grace!

Bestow upon us new blessings. Give to us the freshness of the spring. We are saplings which have been planted by the fingers of Thy bounty and have been formed out of the water and clay of Thy tender affection. We thirst for the living waters of Thy favors and are dependent upon the outpourings of the clouds of Thy generosity. Abandon not to itself this grove wherein our hopes aspire, nor withhold therefrom the showers of Thy loving-kindness. Grant that from the clouds of Thy mercy may fall copious rain so that the trees of our lives may bring forth fruit and we may attain the most cherished desire of our hearts.

—'Abdu'l-Bahá[8]

STRENGTH

Armed with the power of Thy name nothing can ever hurt me, and with Thy love in my heart all the world's afflictions can in no wise alarm me.

—Bahá'u'lláh[1]

Make firm our steps, O Lord, in Thy path and strengthen Thou our hearts in Thine obedience. Turn our faces toward the beauty of Thy oneness, and gladden our bosoms with the signs of Thy divine unity. Adorn our bodies with the robe of Thy bounty, and remove from our eyes the veil of sinfulness, and give us the chalice of Thy grace; that the essence of all beings may sing Thy praise before the vision of Thy grandeur. Reveal then Thyself, O Lord, by Thy merciful utterance and the mystery of Thy divine being, that the holy ecstasy of prayer may fill our souls—a prayer that shall rise above words and letters and transcend the murmur of syllables and sounds—that all things may be merged into nothingness before the revelation of Thy splendor.

Lord! These are servants that have remained fast and firm in Thy Covenant and Thy Testament, that have held fast unto the cord of constancy in Thy Cause and clung unto the hem of the robe of Thy grandeur. Assist them, O Lord, with Thy grace, confirm them with Thy power and strengthen their loins in obedience to Thee.

Thou art the Pardoner, the Gracious.

—'Abdu'l-Bahá[2]

He is God!

O Thou pure God! Let these saplings which have sprouted by the stream of Thy guidance become fresh and verdant through the outpourings of the clouds of Thy tender mercy; cause them to be stirred by the gentle winds wafting from the meads of Thy oneness and suffer them to be revived through the rays of the Sun of Reality, that they may continually grow and flourish, and burst into blossoms and fruit.

O Lord God! Bestow upon each one understanding; give them power and strength and cause them to mirror forth Thy divine aid and confirmation, so that they may become highly distinguished among the people.

Thou art the Mighty and the Powerful.

—'Abdu'l-Bahá[3]

O God, my God! Give me to drink from the cup of Thy bestowal and illumine my face with the light of guidance. Make me firm in the path of faithfulness, assist me to be steadfast in Thy mighty Covenant, and suffer me to be numbered with Thy chosen servants. Unlock before my face the doors of abundance, grant me deliverance, and sustain me, through means I cannot reckon, from the treasuries of heaven. Suffer me to turn my face toward the countenance of Thy generosity and to be entirely devoted to Thee, O Thou Who art merciful and compassionate! To those that stand fast and firm in Thy Covenant Thou, verily, art gracious and generous. All praise be to God, the Lord of the worlds!

—'Abdu'l-Bahá[4]

O Lord! Make this youth radiant, and confer Thy bounty upon this poor creature. Bestow upon him knowledge, grant him added strength at the break of every morn and guard him within the shelter of Thy protection so that he may be freed from error, may devote himself to the service of Thy Cause, may guide the wayward, lead the hapless, free the captives and awaken the heedless, that all may be blessed with Thy remembrance and praise. Thou art the Mighty and the Powerful.

—'Abdu'l-Bahá[5]

LOVE

O Son of Being! Love Me, that I may love thee. If thou lovest Me not, My love can in no wise reach thee. Know this, O servant.

—Bahá'u'lláh[1]

In the love I bear to Thee, O my Lord, my heart longeth for Thee with a longing such as no heart hath known. Here am I with my body between Thy hands, and my spirit before Thy face. Do with them as it may please Thee, for the exaltation of Thy word, and the revelation of what hath been enshrined within the treasuries of Thy knowledge.

Potent art Thou to do what Thou willest, and able to ordain what Thou pleasest.

—Bahá'u'lláh[2]

O Son of Man! I loved thy creation, hence I created thee. Wherefore, do thou love Me, that I may name thy name and fill thy soul with the spirit of life.

—Bahá'u'lláh[3]

T he first sign of faith is love. The message of the holy, divine Manifestations is love; the phenomena of creation are based upon love; the radiance of the world is due to love; the well-being and happiness of the world depend upon it. Therefore, I admonish you that you must strive throughout the human world to diffuse the light of love.

—'Abdu'l-Bahá[4]

W hat a power is love! It is the most wonderful, the greatest of all living powers.

Love gives life to the lifeless. Love lights a flame in the heart that is cold. Love brings hope to the hopeless and gladdens the hearts of the sorrowful.

In the world of existence there is indeed no greater power than the power of love.

—'Abdu'l-Bahá[5]

D o not be content with showing friendship in words alone, let your heart burn with loving kindness for all who may cross your path.

—'Abdu'l-Bahá[6]

G od has created His servants in order that they may love and associate with each other. He has revealed the glorious splendor of His sun of love in the world of humanity. The cause of the creation of the phenomenal world is love.

—'Abdu'l-Bahá[7]

JOY

Send, therefore, unto my loved ones, O my God, what will cheer their hearts, and illumine their faces, and delight their souls. Thou knowest, O my Lord, that their joy is to behold the exaltation of Thy Cause and the glorification of Thy word. Do Thou unveil, therefore, O my God, what will gladden their eyes, and ordain for them the good of this world and of the world which is to come.

Thou art, verily, the God of power, of strength and of bounty.

—Bahá'u'lláh[1]

n this world we are influenced by two sentiments, *Joy* and *Pain.*

Joy gives us wings! In times of joy our strength is more vital, our intellect keener, and our understanding less clouded. We seem better able to cope with the world and to find our sphere of usefulness. But when sadness visits us we become weak, our strength leaves us, our comprehension is dim and our intelligence veiled. The actualities of life seem to elude our grasp, the eyes of our spirits fail to discover the sacred mysteries, and we become even as dead beings.

There is no human being untouched by these two influences; but all the sorrow and the grief that exist come from the world of matter—the spiritual world bestows only the joy!

—'Abdu'l-Bahá[2]

f the heart turns away from the blessings God offers how can it hope for happiness? If it does not put its hope and trust in God's Mercy, where can it find rest? Oh, trust in God! for His Bounty is everlasting, and in His Blessings, for they are superb. Oh! put your faith in the Almighty, for He faileth not and His goodness endureth for ever! His Sun giveth Light continually, and the Clouds of His Mercy are full of the Waters of Compassion with which He waters the hearts of all who trust in Him.

—'Abdu'l-Bahá[3]

May your souls be illumined by the light of the Words of God, and may you become repositories of the mysteries of God, for no comfort is greater and no happiness is sweeter than spiritual comprehension of the divine teachings.

—'Abdu'l-Bahá[4]

True happiness depends on spiritual good and having the heart ever open to receive the Divine Bounty.

—'Abdu'l-Bahá[5]

DIFFICULTIES

Is there any Remover of difficulties save God? Say: Praised be God! He is God! All are His servants, and all abide by His bidding!

—The Báb[1]

I adjure Thee by Thy might, O my God! Let no harm beset me in times of tests, and in moments of heedlessness guide my steps aright through Thine Inspiration. Thou art God, potent art Thou to do what Thou desirest. No one can withstand Thy Will or thwart Thy Purpose.

—The Báb[2]

O God, my God, my Beloved, my heart's Desire.

—The Báb[3]

Tests are benefits from God, for which we should thank Him. Grief and sorrow do not come to us by chance, they are sent to us by the Divine Mercy for our own perfecting.

—'Abdu'l-Bahá[4]

Rely upon God. Trust in Him. Praise Him, and call Him continually to mind. He verily turneth trouble into ease, and sorrow into solace, and toil into utter peace. He verily hath dominion over all things.

—'Abdu'l-Bahá[5]

O Divine Providence! Perplexing difficulties have arisen and formidable obstacles have appeared. O Lord! Remove these difficulties and show forth the evidences of Thy might and power. Ease these hardships and smooth our way along this arduous path. O Divine Providence! The obstacles are unyielding, and our toil and hardship are conjoined with a myriad adversities. There is no helper save Thee, and no succorer except Thyself. We set all our hopes on Thee, and commit all our affairs unto Thy care. Thou art the Guide and the Remover of every difficulty, and Thou art the Wise, the Seeing, and the Hearing.

—'Abdu'l-Bahá[6]

O Lord so rich in bounty, so replete with grace, Whose knowledge doth mine inmost heart and soul embrace!

At morn, the solace of my soul is none but Thee;
The knower of my loss and woe is none but Thee.

The heart that for a moment hath Thy mention known
Will seek no friend save longing pain for Thee alone.

Withered be the heart that sigheth not for Thee,
And better blind the eye that crieth not for Thee!

In all mine hours of deepest gloom, O Lord of might,
My heart hath Thy remembrance for a shining light.

Do, through Thy favour, breathe Thy spirit into
me,
That what hath never been may thus forever be.

Consider not our merit and our worth,
O Lord of bounty, but the grace Thou pourest
forth.

Upon these broken-winged birds whose flight is
slow
Out of Thy tender mercy newfound wings bestow.
—'Abdu'l-Bahá[7]

PROTECTION

I have risen this morning by Thy grace, O my God, and left my home trusting wholly in Thee, and committing myself to Thy care. Send down, then, upon me, out of the heaven of Thy mercy, a blessing from Thy side, and enable me to return home in safety even as Thou didst enable me to set out under Thy protection with my thoughts fixed steadfastly upon Thee.

There is none other God but Thee, the One, the Incomparable, the All-Knowing, the All-Wise.

—Bahá'u'lláh[1]

I have wakened in Thy shelter, O my God, and it becometh him that seeketh that shelter to abide within the Sanctuary of Thy protection and the Stronghold of Thy defense. Illumine my inner being, O my Lord, with the splendors of the Dayspring of Thy Revelation, even as Thou didst illumine my outer being with the morning light of Thy favor.

—Bahá'u'lláh[2]

O God, my God! I have set out from my home, holding fast unto the cord of Thy love, and I have committed myself wholly to Thy care and Thy protection. I entreat Thee by Thy power through which Thou didst protect Thy loved ones from the wayward and the perverse, and from every contumacious oppressor, and every wicked doer who hath strayed far from Thee, to keep me safe by Thy bounty and Thy grace. Enable me, then, to return to my home by Thy power and Thy might. Thou art, truly, the Almighty, the Help in Peril, the Self-Subsisting.

—Bahá'u'lláh[3]

O Son of Utterance! Thou art My stronghold; enter therein that thou mayest abide in safety. My love is in thee, know it, that thou mayest find Me near unto thee.

—Bahá'u'lláh[4]

O God, guide me, protect me, make of me a shining lamp and a brilliant star. Thou art the Mighty and the Powerful.

—'Abdu'l-Bahá[5]

O compassionate God! Thanks be to Thee for Thou hast awakened and made me conscious. Thou hast given me a seeing eye and favored me with a hearing ear, hast led me to Thy kingdom and guided me to Thy path. Thou hast shown me the right way and caused me to enter the ark of deliverance. O God! Keep me steadfast and make me firm and staunch. Protect me from violent tests and preserve and shelter me in the strongly fortified fortress of Thy Covenant and Testament. Thou art the Powerful. Thou art the Seeing. Thou art the Hearing.

O Thou the Compassionate God. Bestow upon me a heart which, like unto a glass, may be illumined with the light of Thy love, and confer upon me thoughts which may change this world into a rose garden through the outpourings of heavenly grace.

Thou art the Compassionate, the Merciful. Thou art the Great Beneficent God.

—'Abdu'l-Bahá[6]

O God, my God! Shield Thy trusted servants from the evils of self and passion, protect them with the watchful eye of Thy loving-kindness from all rancor, hate and envy, shelter them in the impregnable stronghold of Thy care and, safe from the darts of doubtfulness, make them the manifestations of Thy glorious signs, illumine their faces with the effulgent rays shed from the Dayspring of Thy divine unity, gladden their hearts with the verses revealed from Thy holy kingdom, strengthen their loins by Thine all-swaying power that cometh from Thy realm of glory. Thou art the All-Bountiful, the Protector, the Almighty, the Gracious.

—'Abdu'l-Bahá[7]

He is the All-Glorious.

O my Lord, my King, my Ruler, and my Sovereign! I call upon Thee with my tongue, my heart, and my soul, saying: Clothe this servant of Thine with the robe of Thy care, the raiment of Thine unfailing help, and the armour of Thy protection. Assist him to make mention of Thee and to extol Thy virtues amidst Thy people, and unloose his tongue to utter Thy glorification and praise in every assemblage held to celebrate Thy unity and sanctity. Thou art, in truth, the Mighty, the Powerful, the All-Glorious, the Self-Subsisting.

—'Abdu'l-Bahá[8]

HEALING

Thy name is my healing, O my God, and remembrance of Thee is my remedy. Nearness to Thee is my hope, and love for Thee is my companion. Thy mercy to me is my healing and my succor in both this world and the world to come. Thou, verily, art the All-Bountiful, the All-Knowing, the All-Wise.

—Bahá'u'lláh[1]

O Thou Whose tests are a healing medicine to such as are nigh unto Thee, Whose sword is the ardent desire of all them that love Thee, Whose dart is the dearest wish of those hearts that yearn after Thee, Whose decree is the sole hope of them that have recognized Thy truth! I implore Thee, by

Thy divine sweetness and by the splendors of the glory of Thy face, to send down upon us from Thy retreats on high that which will enable us to draw nigh unto Thee. Set, then, our feet firm, O my God, in Thy Cause, and enlighten our hearts with the effulgence of Thy knowledge, and illumine our breasts with the brightness of Thy names.

—Bahá'u'lláh[2]

O Befriended Stranger! The candle of thine heart is lighted by the hand of My power, quench it not with the contrary winds of self and passion. The healer of all thine ills is remembrance of Me, forget it not. Make My love thy treasure and cherish it even as thy very sight and life.

—Baha'u'llah[3]

He is God.
O God, my God! I have set my face towards Thee, and supplicate the outpourings of the ocean of Thy healing. Graciously assist me, O Lord, to serve Thy people and to heal Thy servants. If Thou dost aid me, the remedy I offer will become

a healing medicine for every ailment, a draught of life-giving waters for every burning thirst, and a soothing balm for every yearning heart. If Thou dost not aid me, it will be naught but affliction itself, and I will scarcely bring healing to any soul.

O God, my God! Aid and assist me through Thy power to heal the sick. Thou art, verily, the Healer, the Sufficer, He Who is the remover of every pain and sickness, He Who hath dominion over all things.

—'Abdu'l-Bahá[4]

FORGIVENESS

Turn unto Him, and fear not because of thy deeds. He, in truth, forgiveth whomsoever He desireth as a bounty on His part; no God is there but Him, the Ever-Forgiving, the All-Bounteous.

—Bahá'u'lláh[1]

I beg Thy forgiveness, O my God, and implore pardon after the manner Thou wishest Thy servants to direct themselves to Thee. I beg of Thee to wash away our sins as befitteth Thy Lordship, and to forgive me, my parents, and those who in Thy estimation have entered the abode of Thy love in a manner which is worthy of Thy transcendent sovereignty and well beseemeth the glory of Thy celestial power.

O my God! Thou hast inspired my soul to offer its supplication to Thee, and but for Thee, I would not call upon Thee. Lauded and glorified art Thou; I yield Thee praise inasmuch as Thou didst reveal Thyself unto me, and I beg Thee to forgive me, since I have fallen short in my duty to know Thee and have failed to walk in the path of Thy love.

—The Báb[2]

Praise be unto Thee, O Lord. Forgive us our sins, have mercy upon us and enable us to return unto Thee. Suffer us not to rely on aught else besides Thee, and vouchsafe unto us, through Thy bounty, that which Thou lovest and desirest and well beseemeth Thee. Exalt the station of them that have truly believed, and forgive them with Thy gracious forgiveness. Verily, Thou art the Help in Peril, the Self-Subsisting.

—The Báb[3]

Thy generous Lord will assist thee to labor in His vineyard and will cause thee to be the means of spreading the spirit of unity. . . . He will make thine inner eye to see with the light of knowledge, He will forgive thy sins and transform them into goodly deeds. Verily He is the Forgiving, the Compassionate, the Lord of immeasurable grace.

—'Abdu'l-Bahá[4]

Let not your heart be offended with anyone. If someone commits an error and wrong toward you, you must instantly forgive him. Do not complain of others. Refrain from reprimanding them, and if you wish to give admonition or advice, let it be offered in such a way that it will not burden the bearer. Turn all your thoughts toward bringing joy to hearts. Beware! Beware! Lest ye offend any heart.

—'Abdu'l-Bahá[5]

JUSTICE

Tread ye the path of justice, for this, verily, is the straight path.

—Bahá'u'lláh[1]

I beseech Thee, O my God, by all the transcendent glory of Thy Name, to clothe Thy loved ones in the robe of justice and to illumine their beings with the light of trustworthiness. Thou art the One that hath power to do as He pleaseth and Who holdeth within His grasp the reins of all things, visible and invisible.

—Bahá'u'lláh[2]

O Son of Spirit! The best beloved of all things in My sight is Justice; turn not away therefrom if thou desirest Me, and neglect it not that I may confide in thee. By its aid thou shalt see with thine own eyes and not through the eyes of others, and shalt know of thine own knowledge and not through the knowledge of thy neighbor. Ponder this in thy heart; how it behooveth thee to be. Verily justice is My gift to thee and the sign of My loving-kindness. Set it then before thine eyes.

—Bahá'u'lláh[3]

O God, my God! Attire mine head with the crown of justice, and my temple with the ornament of equity. Thou, verily, art the Possessor of all gifts and bounties.

—Bahá'u'lláh[4]

Oh, friends of God, be living examples of justice! So that by the Mercy of God, the world may see in your actions that you manifest the attributes of justice and mercy.

—'Abdu'l-Bahá[5]

UNITY

Blessed is the spot, and the house, and the place, and the city, and the heart, and the mountain, and the refuge, and the cave, and the valley, and the land, and the sea, and the island, and the meadow where mention of God hath been made, and His praise glorified.

—Bahá'u'lláh[1]

O my God! O my God! Unite the hearts of Thy servants, and reveal to them Thy great purpose. May they follow Thy commandments and abide in Thy law. Help them, O God, in their endeavor, and grant them strength to serve Thee. O God! Leave them not to themselves, but guide their steps by the light of Thy knowledge, and cheer their hearts by Thy love. Verily, Thou art their Helper and their Lord.

—Bahá'u'lláh[2]

O Children of Men! Know ye not why We created you all from the same dust? That no one should exalt himself over the other. Ponder at all times in your hearts how ye were created. Since We have created you all from one same substance it is incumbent on you to be even as one soul, to walk with the same feet, eat with the same mouth and dwell in the same land, that from your inmost being, by your deeds and actions, the signs of oneness and the essence of detachment may be made manifest. Such is My counsel to you, O concourse of light! Heed ye this counsel that ye may obtain the fruit of holiness from the tree of wondrous glory.

—Bahá'u'lláh[3]

O Lord! Enable all the peoples of the earth to gain admittance into the Paradise of Thy

Faith, so that no created being may remain beyond the bounds of Thy good-pleasure.

From time immemorial Thou hast been potent to do what pleaseth Thee and transcendent above whatsoever Thou desirest.

—The Báb[4]

O Thou kind Lord! These are Thy servants who have gathered in this meeting, have turned unto Thy kingdom and are in need of Thy bestowal and blessing. O Thou God! Manifest and make evident the signs of Thy oneness which have been deposited in all the realities of life. Reveal and unfold the virtues which Thou hast made latent and concealed in these human realities.

O God! We are as plants, and Thy bounty is as the rain; refresh and cause these plants to grow through Thy bestowal. We are Thy servants; free us from the fetters of material existence. We are ignorant; make us wise. We are dead; make us alive. We are material; endow us with spirit. We are deprived; make us the intimates of Thy mysteries. We are needy; enrich and bless us from Thy boundless treasury. O God! Resuscitate us; give us sight; give us hearing; familiarize us with the mysteries of life, so that the secrets of Thy kingdom may become revealed to us in this world of existence and we may confess Thy oneness. Every bestowal emanates from Thee; every benediction is Thine.

Thou art mighty. Thou art powerful. Thou art the Giver, and Thou art the Ever-Bounteous.

—'Abdu'l-Bahá[5]

O Thou compassionate Lord, Thou Who art generous and able! We are servants of Thine sheltered beneath Thy providence. Cast Thy glance of favor upon us. Give light to our eyes, hearing to our ears, and understanding and love to our hearts. Render our souls joyous and happy through Thy glad tidings. O Lord! Point out to us the pathway of Thy kingdom and resuscitate all of us through the breaths of the Holy Spirit. Bestow upon us life everlasting and confer upon us never-ending honor. Unify mankind and illumine the world of humanity. May we all follow Thy pathway, long for Thy good pleasure and seek the mysteries of Thy kingdom. O God! Unite us and connect our hearts with Thy indissoluble bond. Verily, Thou art the Giver, Thou art the Kind One and Thou art the Almighty.

—'Abdu'l-Bahá[6]

O my God! O my God! Verily, these servants are turning to Thee, supplicating Thy kingdom of mercy. Verily, they are attracted by Thy holiness and set aglow with the fire of Thy love, seeking confirmation from Thy wondrous kingdom, and hoping for attainment in Thy heavenly realm. Verily, they long for the descent of Thy bestowal, desiring illumination from the Sun of Reality. O Lord! Make them radiant lamps, merciful signs, fruitful trees and shining stars. May they come forth in Thy service and be connected with Thee by the bonds and ties of Thy love, longing for the lights of Thy favor. O Lord! Make them signs of guidance, standards of Thine immortal kingdom, waves of the sea of Thy mercy, mirrors of the light of Thy majesty.

Verily, Thou art the Generous. Verily, Thou art the Merciful. Verily, Thou art the Precious, the Beloved.

—'Abdu'l-Bahá[7]

O Thou kind Lord! Thou hast created all humanity from the same stock. Thou hast decreed that all shall belong to the same household. In Thy Holy Presence they are all Thy servants, and all mankind are sheltered beneath Thy Tabernacle; all have gathered together at Thy Table of Bounty; all are illumined through the light of Thy Providence.

O God! Thou art kind to all, Thou hast provided for all, dost shelter all, conferrest life upon all. Thou hast endowed each and all with talents and faculties, and all are submerged in the Ocean of Thy Mercy.

O Thou kind Lord! Unite all. Let the religions agree and make the nations one, so that they may see each other as one family and the whole earth as one home. May they all live together in perfect harmony.

O God! Raise aloft the banner of the oneness of mankind.

O God! Establish the Most Great Peace.

Cement Thou, O God, the hearts together.

O Thou kind Father, God! Gladden our hearts through the fragrance of Thy love. Brighten our eyes through the Light of Thy Guidance. Delight our ears with the melody of Thy Word, and shelter us all in the Stronghold of Thy Providence.

Thou art the Mighty and Powerful, Thou art the Forgiving and Thou art the One Who overlooketh the shortcomings of all mankind.

—'Abdu'l-Bahá[8]

You must manifest complete love and affection toward all mankind. Do not exalt yourselves above others, but consider all as your equals, recognizing them as the servants of one God. Know that God is compassionate toward all; therefore, love all from the depths of your hearts, prefer all religionists before yourselves, be filled with love for every race, and be kind toward the people of all nationalities.

—'Abdu'l-Bahá[9]

SERVICE

O brethren! Let deeds, not words, be your adorning.

—Bahá'u'lláh[1]

Service to humanity is service to God.

—'Abdu'l-Bahá[2]

O Thou kind Lord! Graciously bestow a pair of heavenly wings unto each of these fledglings, and give them spiritual power that they may wing their flight through this limitless space and may soar to the heights of the Abhá Kingdom.

O Lord! Strengthen these fragile seedlings that each one may become a fruitful tree, verdant and flourishing. Render these souls victorious through the potency of Thy celestial hosts, that they may be able to crush the forces of error and ignorance and to unfurl the standard of fellowship and guidance amidst the people; that they may, even as the reviving breaths of the spring, refresh and quicken the trees of human souls and like unto vernal showers make the meads of that region green and fertile.

Thou art the Mighty and the Powerful; Thou art the Bestower and the All-Loving.

—'Abdu'l-Bahá[3]

O my God, aid Thou Thy servant to raise up the Word, and to refute what is vain and false, to establish the truth, to spread the sacred verses abroad, reveal the splendors, and make the morning's light to dawn in the hearts of the righteous.

Thou art, verily, the Generous, the Forgiving.

—'Abdu'l-Bahá[4]

O God, my God! Aid Thou Thy trusted servants to have loving and tender hearts. Help them to spread, amongst all the nations of the earth, the light of guidance that cometh from the Company on high. Verily, Thou art the Strong, the Powerful, the Mighty, the All-Subduing, the Ever-Giving. Verily, Thou art the Generous, the Gentle, the Tender, the Most Bountiful.

—'Abdu'l-Bahá[5]

This is worship: to serve mankind and to minister to the needs of the people. Service is prayer.

—'Abdu'l-Bahá[6]

If a soul be ailing and infirm, we must produce remedies; if ignorant, we must provide education; if defective, we must train and perfect that which is lacking; if immature and undeveloped, we must supply the means of attainment to maturity. No soul should be hated, none neglected; nay, rather, their very imperfections should demand greater kindness and tender compassion. Therefore, if we follow the example of the Lord of divinity, we will love all mankind from our hearts, and the means of the unity of the world of humanity

will become as evident and manifest to us as the
light of the sun.

—'Abdu'l-Bahá[7]

ARTS & SCIENCES

Arts, crafts and sciences uplift the world of being, and are conducive to its exaltation.

—Bahá'u'lláh[1]

Knowledge is one of the wondrous gifts of God. It is incumbent upon everyone to acquire it. Such arts and material means as are now manifest have been achieved by virtue of His knowledge and wisdom which have been revealed in Epistles and Tablets through His Most Exalted Pen—a Pen out of whose treasury pearls of wisdom and utterance and the arts and crafts of the world are brought to light.

—Bahá'u'lláh[2]

One of the names of God is the Fashioner. He loveth craftsmanship. Therefore any of His servants who manifesteth this attribute is acceptable in the sight of this Wronged One. Craftsmanship is a book among the books of divine sciences, and a treasure among the treasures of His heavenly wisdom. This is a knowledge with meaning, for some of the sciences are brought forth by words and come to an end with words.

—Bahá'u'lláh[3]

Exert your utmost endeavor that ye may develop such crafts and undertakings that everyone, whether young or old, may benefit therefrom.

—Bahá'u'lláh[4]

The acquisition of sciences and the perfection of arts are considered acts of worship.

—'Abdu'l-Bahá[5]

In this wonderful new age, art is worship. The more thou strivest to perfect it, the closer wilt thou come to God. What bestowal could be greater than this, that one's art should be even as the act of worshipping the Lord? That is to say, when thy fingers grasp the paintbrush, it is as if thou wert at prayer in the Temple.

—'Abdu'l-Bahá[6]

May you become learned in sciences, acquire the arts and crafts, prove to be useful members of human society and assist the progress of human civilization. May you be a cause of the manifestation of divine bestowals—each one of you a shining star radiating the light of the oneness of humanity toward the horizons of the East and West. May you be devoted to the love and unity of mankind, and through your efforts may the reality deposited in the human heart find its divine expression.

—'Abdu'l-Bahá[7]

CHILDREN

O Compassionate God! O Lord of Hosts! Praise be unto Thee that Thou hast preferred these little children over the full-grown and mature, and bestowed upon them Thy special favors. Thou hast guided them. Thou hast been kind to them. Thou hast conferred upon them illumination and spirituality. Grant us Thy confirmation so that, when we grow up, we may engage in service to Thy Kingdom, become the cause of educating others, burn like radiant candles and shine like brilliant stars. Thou art the Giver, the Bestower, the Compassionate.

—'Abdu'l-Bahá[1]

O God! Educate these children. These children are the plants of Thine orchard, the flowers of Thy meadow, the roses of Thy garden. Let Thy rain fall upon them; let the Sun of Reality shine upon them with Thy love. Let Thy breeze refresh them in order that they may be trained, grow and develop, and appear in the utmost beauty. Thou art the Giver. Thou art the Compassionate.

—'Abdu'l-Bahá[2]

O Thou kind Lord! These lovely children are the handiwork of the fingers of Thy might and the wondrous signs of Thy greatness. O God! Protect these children, graciously assist them to be educated and enable them to render service to the world of humanity. O God! These children are pearls, cause them to be nurtured within the shell of Thy loving-kindness.

Thou art the Bountiful, the All-Loving.

—'Abdu'l-Bahá[3]

O Lord!

Plant this tender seedling in the garden of Thy manifold bounties, water it from the fountains of Thy loving-kindness and grant that it may grow into a goodly plant through the outpourings of Thy favor and grace.

Thou art the Mighty and the Powerful.

—'Abdu'l-Bahá[4]

PARENTS

S how honor to your parents and pay homage to them. This will cause blessings to descend upon you from the clouds of the bounty of your Lord, the Exalted, the Great.

—Bahá'u'lláh[1]

O Divine Providence! Immerse the father and mother of this servant of Thy Threshold in the ocean of Thy forgiveness, and purge and sanctify them from every sin and transgression. Grant them Thy forgiveness and mercy, and bestow upon them Thy gracious pardon. Thou, verily, art the Pardoner, the Ever-Forgiving, the Bestower of abundant grace. O Thou forgiving Lord! Though we are sinners, yet our hopes are fixed upon Thy promise and assurance. Though we are enveloped by the darkness of error, yet we have at all times turned our faces to the morn of Thy bountiful favours. Deal with us as beseemeth Thy Threshold, and confer upon us that which is worthy of Thy Court. Thou art the Ever-Forgiving, the Pardoner, He Who overlooketh every shortcoming.

—'Abdu'l-Bahá[2]

O Thou forgiving God! Forgive the sins of my loving mother, pardon her shortcomings, cast upon her the glance of Thy gracious providence, and enable her to gain admittance into Thy Kingdom.

O God! From the earliest days of my life she educated and nurtured me, yet I did not recompense her for her toil and labors. Do Thou reward her by granting her eternal life and making her exalted in Thy Kingdom.

Verily, Thou art the Forgiver, the Bestower, and the Kind.

—'Abdu'l-Bahá[3]

O Lord! In this Most Great Dispensation Thou dost accept the intercession of children in behalf of their parents. This is one of the special infinite bestowals of this Dispensation. Therefore, O Thou kind Lord, accept the request of this Thy servant at the threshold of Thy singleness and submerge his father in the ocean of Thy grace, because this son hath arisen to render Thee service and is exerting effort at all times in the pathway of Thy love. Verily, Thou art the Giver, the Forgiver and the Kind!

—'Abdu'l-Bahá[4]

PRAYERS SPECIFICALLY FOR GIRLS

O Lord!

Help this daughter of the Kingdom to be exalted in both worlds; cause her to turn away from this mortal world of dust and from those who have set their hearts thereon and enable her to have communion and close association with the world of immortality. Give her heavenly power and strengthen her through the breaths of the Holy Spirit that she may arise to serve Thee.

Thou art the Mighty One.

—'Abdu'l-Bahá

O Thou kind Lord! Bestow heavenly confirmation upon this daughter of the kingdom, and graciously aid her that she may remain firm and steadfast in Thy Cause and that she may, even as a nightingale of the rose garden of mysteries, warble melodies in the Abhá Kingdom in the most wondrous tones, thereby bringing happiness to everyone. Make her exalted among the daughters of the kingdom and enable her to attain life eternal.

Thou art the Bestower, the All-Loving.

—'Abdu'l-Bahá[2]

O my Lord, my Beloved, my Desire! Befriend me in my loneliness and accompany me in my exile. Remove my sorrow. Cause me to be devoted to Thy beauty. Withdraw me from all else save Thee. Attract me through Thy fragrances of holiness. Cause me to be associated in Thy Kingdom with those who are severed from all else save Thee, who long to serve Thy sacred threshold and who stand to work in Thy Cause. Enable me to be one of Thy maidservants who have attained to Thy good pleasure. Verily, Thou art the Gracious, the Generous.

—'Abdu'l-Bahá[3]

FOR THOSE WHO HAVE PASSED AWAY

O Son of the Supreme! I have made death a messenger of joy to thee. Wherefore dost thou grieve? I made the light to shed on thee its splendor. Why dost thou veil thyself therefrom?

—Bahá'u'lláh[1]

O my God! O Thou forgiver of sins, bestower of gifts, dispeller of afflictions! Verily, I beseech thee to forgive the sins of such as have abandoned the physical garment and have ascended to the spiritual world.

O my Lord! Purify them from trespasses, dispel their sorrows, and change their darkness into light. Cause them to enter the garden of happiness, cleanse them with the most pure water, and grant them to behold Thy splendors on the loftiest mount.

—'Abdu'l-Bahá[2]

O Thou Provider, O Thou Forgiver! A noble soul hath ascended unto the Kingdom of reality, and hastened from the mortal world of dust to the realm of everlasting glory. Exalt the station of this recently arrived guest, and attire this long-standing servant with a new and wondrous robe.

O Thou Peerless Lord! Grant Thy forgiveness and tender care so that this soul may be admitted into the retreats of Thy mysteries and may become an intimate companion in the assemblage of splendours. Thou art the Giver, the Bestower, the Ever-Loving. Thou art the Pardoner, the Tender, the Most Powerful.

—'Abdu'l-Bahá[3]

SHORT OBLIGATORY PRAYER

I bear witness, O my God, that Thou hast created me to know Thee and to worship Thee.

I testify, at this moment, to my powerlessness and to Thy might, to my poverty and to Thy wealth.

There is none other God but Thee, the Help in Peril, the Self-Subsisting.

—Bahá'u'lláh[1]

GLOSSARY

Abhá Kingdom: The Most Glorious Kingdom, a Bahá'í phrase indicating the next world, the realm of souls.

Abhá Paradise: The Most Glorious Paradise, a Bahá'í phrase indicating the next world, the realm of souls.

Abode: home, house, or residence.

Acquire: to get, come into possession; to come to have as a new characteristic, trait, or ability.

Acquisition: the act of acquiring or getting something.

Adjure: to urge or request.

Affliction: pain, suffering, or illness.

Ark of Deliverance: a reference to the Bahá'í Covenant; spiritual salvation.

Ascend: to go up, rise; a way to describe a soul going to the next world.

Assemblage: a gathering.

Attire: clothes, clothing.

Attribute: a quality or characteristic.

Befitteth: to be appropriate for.

Behooveth: a responsibility for someone to do something, a duty.

Beloved: a reference to Bahá'u'lláh or God when capitalized.

Beneficent: generous, doing good.

Bestow / Bestowal: to give; the act of giving an honor or gift.

Bounty / Bounties / Bounteous: abundance; blessings; generously given.

Brethren: brothers, people belonging to a particular group.

Chalice: a large cup or goblet.

Commemoration: remembrance.

Company on High: a group of souls in the next world, angels.

Concourse: a crowd or assembly of people.

Confer / Conferrest / Conferred: to grant, bestow, give.

Contumacious: stubbornly or willfully disobedient, rebellious.

Counsel: advice.

Countenance: face, expression.

Covenant: an agreement or promise.

Dayspring: the beginning of a new era or order of things, a new day, dawn.

Daystar: morning star.

Detachment: separation, indifference to worldly concerns, freedom from the material world.

Dispensation: an era or epoch, a period of time for a religion or revelation.

Dominion: domain, sovereignty, ownership, authority.

Effulgent / Effulgence: brilliant, shining forth; radiance.

Endeavor: to attempt something, to strive for, exertion or effort.

Enshrine: to enclose, to preserve or cherish.

Epistle: a letter.

Eventide: evening, close of the day.

Exalt: to elevate, praise, glorify.

Exert: to put forth effort, to put oneself into action.

Extol: to praise highly.

Fetters: a chain or shackle; something that confines or restrains.

Fledgling: a young bird; an immature or inexperienced person.

Hapless: unfortunate, having no luck.

Heedless: inconsiderate, thoughtless, lacking concern, careless.

Homage: expression of high regard, show of respect to another.

Hyacinth: a type of flower.

Incumbent: obligatory, a duty.

Indissoluble: permanent, enduring, unbreakable, not removable.

Intercession: prayer, petition, entreaty in favor of another.

Latent: not visible or obvious now but capable of growing or emerging in the future.

Laud / Lauded: praise, extol; glorified.

Loftiest mount: High location.

Maidservant: a female servant.

Manifest: to make evident, show, or display; readily perceived.

Manifold: many, marked by variety.

Meads: meadows.

Most Great Peace: a time when the earth will be transformed, when all the social problems will give way to peace and tranquility. The Bahá'í Writings say this will take place during the Golden Age, a time in the future when society reaches the final stage of the Bahá'í Era.

Naught: nothing.

Nigh: near, close, almost; near in time or place.

Peril: danger, risk.

Refuge: shelter, protection.

Repository: a place or container where something is stored.

Revelation: Something that is communicated from God to humans, often through an intermediary referred to as a Prophet or Manifestation of God.

Sanctify: purify; to set apart for a sacred use.

Sovereignty: a supreme power, a controlling influence.

Splendor: brilliance, magnificence, a great luster or glow.

Staunch: steadfast in loyalty or principle.

Steadfast: firm in belief, determination, or adherence; loyal.

Strive: to devote serious effort or energy.

Succor / Succorer: relief, aid; one who provides help.

Sufficing / Sufficer: to be enough for; one who meets or satisfies a need.

Sun of Reality: a reference to Bahá'u'lláh or God.

Supplicate: to pray; to ask humbly.

Tabernacle: a house of worship, a sanctuary, a dwelling place, a receptacle for sacred elements.

Tablet: A letter, divinely revealed scripture.

Testament: a covenant between God and humanity; a proof or tribute; an expression of conviction.

Threshold: door, gate, an end or boundary, the place or point of entering or beginning.

Thine: an archaic way of saying "yours"; the one addressed.

Thou: an archaic way of saying "you"; the one addressed.

Thy: an archaic way of saying "your"; the one addressed.

Transcendent: exceeding usual limits, beyond ordinary experience, surpassing, beyond comprehension.

Tread: to step or walk, proceed along.

Verdant: green, with growing plants.

Warble: to sing, a melodious or pleasing sound, a musical trill.

Wayward: following one's depraved inclinations, following no clear principle or law, opposite of what is desired or expected.

Wherefore: therefore, for that reason; why, for what reason or purpose.

NOTES

Epigraph
1. 'Abdu'l-Bahá, *Paris Talks*, no. 26.7.

Giving Thanks
1. Bahá'u'lláh, *Tablets of Bahá'u'lláh*, no. 3.20.
2. Bahá'u'lláh, Additional Prayers Revealed by Bahá'u'lláh, https://www.bahai.org/library/authoritative-texts/bahaullah/additional-prayers-revealed-bahaullah/294938659/1#908556715.
3. 'Abdu'l-Bahá, *The Promulgation of Universal Peace*, p. 262.
4. 'Abdu'l-Bahá, *Selections from the Writings of 'Abdu'l-Bahá*, no. 2.18.
5. 'Abdu'l-Bahá, *Selections from the Writings of 'Abdu'l-Bahá*, no. 6.2–3.

Trust in God

1. Bahá'u'lláh, in *The Dawn-Breakers,* p. 632.
2. Bahá'u'lláh, Additional Prayers Revealed by Bahá'u'lláh, https://www.bahai.org/library/authoritative-texts/bahaullah/additional-prayers-revealed-bahaullah/182178792/1#533738942.
3. The Báb, in *Bahá'í Prayers,* p. 56.
4. The Báb, in *Bahá'í Prayers,* pp. 55–56.
5. 'Abdu'l-Bahá, *Pearls of Bounty,* no. 1.15.1–3.

Spiritual Growth

1. Bahá'u'lláh, in *Bahá'í Prayers,* p. 162.
2. Bahá'u'lláh, in *Bahá'í Prayers,* p. 164.
3. 'Abdu'l-Bahá, in *Bahá'í Prayers,* p. 29.
4. 'Abdu'l-Bahá, in *Bahá'í Prayers,* p. 69.
5. 'Abdu'l-Bahá, *Pearls of Bounty,* no. 1.1.1–2.
6. 'Abdu'l-Bahá, *Pearls of Bounty,* no. 1.2.1–2.
7. 'Abdu'l-Bahá, *Pearls of Bounty,* no. 1.5.1–2.
8. 'Abdu'l-Bahá, *Pearls of Bounty,* no. 1.7.1–2.

Strength

1. Bahá'u'lláh, in *Bahá'í Prayers,* p. 142.
2. 'Abdu'l-Bahá, in *Bahá'í Prayers,* p. 68.
3. 'Abdu'l-Bahá, *Pearls of Bounty,* no. 1.4.1–3.

4. 'Abdu'l-Bahá, *Pearls of Bounty,* no. 1.16.1.
5. 'Abdu'l-Bahá, in *Bahá'í Prayers,* p. 248.

Love

1. Bahá'u'lláh, The Hidden Words, Arabic, no. 5.
2. Bahá'u'lláh, *Prayers and Meditations by Bahá'u'lláh,* no. 151.3–4.
3. Bahá'u'lláh, The Hidden Words, Arabic, no. 4.
4. 'Abdu'l-Bahá, *The Promulgation of Universal Peace,* p. 477.
5. 'Abdu'l-Bahá, *Paris Talks,* no. 58.1–3.
6. 'Abdu'l-Bahá, *Paris Talks,* no. 1.7.
7. 'Abdu'l-Bahá, *The Promulgation of Universal Peace,* p. 414.

Joy

1. Bahá'u'lláh, *Prayers and Meditations by Bahá'u'lláh,* no. 114.8–9.
2. 'Abdu'l-Bahá, *Paris Talks,* no. 35.1–3.
3. 'Abdu'l-Bahá, *Paris Talks,* no. 34.8.
4. 'Abdu'l-Bahá, *The Promulgation of Universal Peace,* pp. 648–49.
5. 'Abdu'l-Bahá, *Paris Talks,* no. 34.7.

Difficulties

1. The Báb, in *Bahá'í Prayers,* p. 221.
2. The Báb, in *Bahá'í Prayers,* p. 223.
3. The Báb, in *Bahá'í Prayers,* p. 129.
4. 'Abdu'l-Bahá, *Paris Talks,* no. 14.7.
5. 'Abdu'l-Bahá, *Selections from the Writings of 'Abdu'l-Bahá,* no. 150.3.
6. 'Abdu'l-Bahá, *Eternal Beloved,* no. 6.
7. 'Abdu'l-Bahá, *Eternal Beloved,* no. 26.

Protection

1. Bahá'u'lláh, in *Bahá'í Prayers,* p. 122.
2. Bahá'u'lláh, in *Bahá'í Prayers,* pp. 121–22.
3. Bahá'u'lláh, in *Bahá'í Prayers,* p. 144.
4. Bahá'u'lláh, The Hidden Words, Arabic, no. 10.
5. 'Abdu'l-Bahá, in *Bahá'í Prayers,* p. 29.
6. 'Abdu'l-Bahá, in *Bahá'í Prayers,* p. 69.
7. 'Abdu'l-Bahá, in *Bahá'í Prayers,* p. 150.
8. 'Abdu'l-Bahá, *Eternal Beloved,* no. 20.

Healing

1. Bahá'u'lláh, in *Bahá'í Prayers,* p. 94.
2. Bahá'u'lláh, in *Bahá'í Prayers,* p. 216.

3. Bahá'u'lláh, The Hidden Words, Persian, no. 32.
4. 'Abdu'l-Bahá, *Eternal Beloved,* no. 9.

Forgiveness

1. Bahá'u'lláh, The Kitáb-i-Aqdas, ¶184.
2. The Báb, in *Bahá'í Prayers,* pp. 62–63.
3. The Báb, in *Bahá'í Prayers,* pp. 77–78.
4. 'Abdu'l-Bahá, *Selections from the Writings of 'Abdu'l-Bahá,* no. 141.6.
5. 'Abdu'l-Bahá, *The Promulgation of Universal Peace,* pp. 63–69.

Justice

1. Bahá'u'lláh, *Gleanings from the Writings of Bahá'u'lláh,* no. 118.1.
2. Bahá'u'lláh, in *Bahá'í Prayers,* p. 170.
3. Bahá'u'lláh, The Hidden Words, Arabic, no. 2.
4. Bahá'u'lláh, *Epistle to the Son of the Wolf,* pp. 12–13.
5. 'Abdu'l-Bahá, *Paris Talks,* no. 49.14.

Unity

1. Bahá'u'lláh, in *Bahá'í Prayers,* p. i.
2. Bahá'u'lláh, in *Bahá'í Prayers,* p. 233.

3. Bahá'u'lláh, The Hidden Words, Arabic, no. 68.

4. The Báb, in *Bahá'í Prayers,* p. 229.

5. 'Abdu'l-Bahá, in *Bahá'í Prayers,* pp. 86–87.

6. 'Abdu'l-Bahá, in *Bahá'í Prayers,* p. 110.

7. 'Abdu'l-Bahá, in *Bahá'í Prayers,* pp. 87–88.

8. 'Abdu'l-Bahá, in *Bahá'í Prayers,* pp. 112–13.

9. 'Abdu'l-Bahá, *The Promulgation of Universal Peace,* p. 638.

Service

1. Bahá'u'lláh, The Hidden Words, Persian, no. 5.

2. 'Abdu'l-Bahá, *The Promulgation of Universal Peace,* p. 10.

3. 'Abdu'l-Bahá, in *Bahá'í Prayers,* pp. 246–47.

4. 'Abdu'l-Bahá, in *Bahá'í Prayers,* p. 197–98.

5. 'Abdu'l-Bahá, in *Bahá'í Prayers,* p. 198.

6. 'Abdu'l-Bahá, *Paris Talks,* no. 55.1.

7. 'Abdu'l-Bahá, *The Promulgation of Universal Peace,* p. 448.

Arts & Sciences

1. Bahá'u'lláh, *Epistle to the Son of the Wolf,* p. 26.

2. Bahá'u'lláh, *Tablets of Bahá'u'lláh*, no. 4.23.
3. Bahá'u'lláh, in *Pause & Reflect: Meditations for Creativity*, p. 40. See Bahá'í Reference Library.
4. Bahá'u'lláh, *Tablets of Bahá'u'lláh*, no. 9.41.
5. 'Abdu'l-Bahá, *Selections from the Writings of 'Abdu'l-Bahá*, no. 126.1.
6. 'Abdu'l-Bahá, in *Pause & Reflect: Meditations for Creativity*, p. 13. See Bahá'í Reference Library.
7. 'Abdu'l-Bahá, *The Promulgation of Universal Peace*, p. 127.

Children
1. 'Abdu'l-Bahá, *Pearls of Bounty*, no. 1.14.1.
2. 'Abdu'l-Bahá, in *Bahá'í Prayers*, p. 28.
3. 'Abdu'l-Bahá, in *Bahá'í Prayers*, p. 28.
4. 'Abdu'l-Bahá, *Pearls of Bounty*, no 1.1–2.

Parents
1. Bahá'u'lláh, in *Family Life*, no. 44.
2. 'Abdu'l-Bahá, *Eternal Beloved*, no. 13.
3. 'Abdu'l-Bahá, *Pearls of Bounty*, no. 1.19.1–3.
4. 'Abdu'l-Bahá, in *Bahá'í Prayers*, p. 63.

Prayers Specifically for Girls

1. 'Abdu'l-Bahá, *Pearls of Bounty,* no. 1.5.1–2.
2. 'Abdu'l-Bahá, in *Bahá'í Prayers,* pp. 247–48.
3. 'Abdu'l-Bahá, in *Bahá'í Prayers,* pp. 243–44.

For the Departed

1. Bahá'u'lláh, The Hidden Words, Arabic, no. 32.
2. 'Abdu'l-Bahá, in *Bahá'í Prayers,* p. 40.
3. 'Abdu'l-Bahá, *Eternal Beloved,* no. 11.

Special Prayer – Short Obligatory Prayer

1. Bahá'u'lláh, in *Bahá'í Prayers,* p. 4.

BIBLIOGRAPHY

Works of Bahá'u'lláh

Epistle to the Son of the Wolf. New ed. Translated by Shoghi Effendi. 1st ps ed. Wilmette, IL: Bahá'í Publishing Trust, 1988.

Gleanings from the Writings of Bahá'u'lláh. Translated by Shoghi Effendi. Wilmette, IL: Bahá'í Publishing, 2005.

The Hidden Words. Translated by Shoghi Effendi. Wilmette, IL: Bahá'í Publishing, 2002.

The Kitáb-i-Aqdas: The Most Holy Book. 1st ps ed. Wilmette, IL: Bahá'í Publishing Trust, 1993.

Prayers and Meditations by Bahá'u'lláh. Translated by Shoghi Effendi. Wilmette, IL: Bahá'í Publishing, 2016.

Tablets of Bahá'u'lláh revealed after the Kitáb-i-Aqdas. Compiled by the Research Department of the Universal House of Justice. Translated by Habib Taherzadeh et al. Wilmette, IL: Bahá'í Publishing Trust, 1988.

Works of 'Abdu'l-Bahá

Eternal Beloved: Prayers of 'Abdu'l-Bahá. Wilmette, IL: Bahá'í Publishing, 2021.

Paris Talks: Addresses Given By 'Abdu'l-Bahá in Paris in 1911. Wilmette, IL: Bahá'í Publishing, 2011.

Pearls of Bounty: Selections from the Prayers, Tablets, and Talks of 'Abdu'l-Bahá. Wilmette, IL: Bahá'í Publishing, 2021.

Promulgation of Universal Peace: Talks Delivered by 'Abdu'l-Bahá during His Visit to the United States and Canada in 1912. Compiled by Howard MacNutt. Wilmette, IL: Bahá'í Publishing, 2012.

Selections from the Writings of 'Abdu'l-Bahá. Compiled by the Research Department of the Universal House of Justice. Translated by a Committee at the Bahá'í World Center and Marzieh Gail. Wilmette, IL: Bahá'í Publishing, 2010.

Bahá'í Compilations and Other Works

Bahá'í Prayers: A Selection of Prayers Revealed by Bahá'u'lláh, the Báb, and 'Abdu'l-Bahá. New ed. Wilmette, IL: Bahá'í Publishing Trust, 2002.

Nábil-i-A'ẓam [Muḥammad-i-Zarandí]. *The Dawn-Breakers: Nabíl's Narrative of the Early Days of the Bahá'í Revelation.* Translated and edited by Shoghi Effendi. Wilmette, IL: Bahá'í Publishing Trust, 1999.

Pause and Reflect: Meditations for Creativity. Wilmette, IL: Bahá'í Publishing, 2020.